## THE LANTERN BEARERS SERIES

When the night is darkest, there are always those who hold up a lantern to light the way.

**Book 1: The Lamp of Education**
*The Winter Plum: How Wu Yifang Became the First Woman to Sign the UN Charter*

From bound feet in 1893 China to the United Nations in 1945, Wu Yifang bloomed like a winter plum—fearless in frost, fragrant and strong. She became China's first female PhD in Biology, led Ginling College through World War II, and became the first woman to sign the UN Charter. Her lamp of education lit the way for generations.

**Book 2: The Lamp of Compassion**
*The Sheltering Tree: How Minnie Vautrin Saved 10,000 Lives in Wartime China*

When darkness fell on Nanjing in 1937, Minnie Vautrin became a sheltering tree, her branches wide enough to protect ten thousand women and children. The "Goddess of Nanking" stood between soldiers and refugees, risking her life daily. Her lamp of compassion burned through the darkest nights.

**Book 3: The Lamp of Truth**
*The Iris Blooms: How Iris Chang Revealed the Truth About the Nanjing Massacre*

Like the iris flower—her namesake—Iris Chang bloomed in defiance, revealing truths the world had forgotten. Her groundbreaking book *The Rape of Nanking* (1997) broke sixty years of silence and awakened global awareness. Her lamp of truth continues to shine, reminding us that memory is an act of justice.

Three women. Three flowers. Three lamps. Together, they prove that even a single flame can drive away the darkness.
May their light inspire you to be brave, to be kind, and to stand for truth.

# The Iris Blooms

## How Iris Chang Revealed the Truth About the Nanjing Massacre

Written by
TAN FENGXIA

Illustrated by
LIANG PEILING

Books Beyond Boundaries
ROYAL COLLINS

The Iris Blooms: How Iris Chang Revealed the Truth About the Nanjing Massacre

Book 3 of *The Lantern Bearers Series*

Writer: Tan Fengxia
Acquisitions editor: Yu Xiaohua
Illustrator: Liang Peiling
Translator: Sun Qingyue

First published in 2026 by Royal Collins Publishing Group Inc.
Groupe Publication Royal Collins Inc.
550-555 boul. René-Lévesque O Montréal (Québec) H2Z1B1 Canada

10 9 8 7 6 5 4 3 2 1



Originally published in Chinese as《正义之灯：张纯如的故事》



ISBN: 978-1-4878-1387-1

To find out more about our publications, please visit www.royalcollins.com.

In memory of Iris Chang (1968–2004), who gave the voiceless a voice,
and lit a lamp that will never go dark.

Special thanks to Professor Ying-Ying Chang, Iris's mother,
for her generous support and trust in this project.

Her memoir, *The Woman Who Could Not Forget*,
was an essential reference.

Spring, 1968. Iris Chang was born in Princeton, New Jersey.

Her parents had just earned their PhDs from Harvard and were doing research at Princeton University. The arrival of this little one brought both busyness and joy.

Little Iris began to toddle. The green lawns of the campus witnessed her first brave steps.

"Shun-Ru, well done," her mother encouraged softly.

"Iris, come on!" her father called out in delight.

Even before she was born, her parents had chosen a beautiful name for her.

Her Chinese name, Shun-Ru (纯如), means "Pure and Innocent."

Her English name, Iris, comes from the rainbow goddess in Greek mythology. It is also the iris of the eye that helps people see the world clearly, and the iris flower—a symbol of faith and hope.

The family moved to the vast plains of Champaign, Illinois. In this quiet "Cornfield" town, Iris ran free under the American sky. But inside her home, China was always present.

"Why must I learn Chinese?" Iris asked.

"Because we are Chinese," her mother said. "These are your roots."

Grandfather unfolded a map. He pointed to the Great Wall, coiling like a giant dragon. He traced the Yangtze River, flowing through his memories.

Iris touched the paper lines. She dreamed of the day she would see the dragon for herself.

When her father returned from a trip to China, he brought home fascinating Chinese storybooks. Her parents read aloud myths and folktales, and Iris listened with rapt attention.

"I'm Sun Wukong, causing havoc in Heaven!" her mischievous brother declared, imitating the Monkey King.

"I'm Hua Mulan, fighting off enemy armies!" Iris preferred playing the brave heroine.

Her weapon was not a sword. It was words.

Her father also brought back sheets of silkworm eggs. The family began raising silkworms.

Iris invited her American friends to watch the silkworms munch mulberry leaves and spin their cocoons.

"Look—it's coming out! The silkworm's turning into a moth!" she cried excitedly. "It must take so much strength to chew through the cocoon!"

She even wrote a poem: "A poem ... is a spring silkworm spinning its cocoon." She imagined the rich silk-producing villages along the Yangtze River—they must be idyllic and picturesque.

Spring brought weekend adventures. The family scooped tadpoles from the creek.

"Look! Legs are growing!" Iris cried. "The tail is getting shorter!"

"Let's take him back to the river," she said gently. Every creature needed its home.

She even gave small creatures a voice in her stories. While her kitten purred nearby, she created *The Mouse Gazette*—a newspaper where the smallest citizens had the biggest adventures.

Just like the silkworm spinning silk, Iris was learning to spin words. Someday, she would write for the world. But she would never forget: Every voice matters.

Iris lived in a world of books and thoughts. In Grade Three, the class studied American heroes. Iris didn't pick a general. She picked Clara Barton, the "Angel of the Battlefield."

Dressed as a nurse, she told her mother why: "She was brave. She didn't run away from the war; she ran toward the wounded."

Her mother looked at her eight-year-old daughter. She saw a spark of that same fire.

TIME

Growing up in American culture, Iris felt a longing to find her "roots."

One evening at dinner, as she picked up the Chinese dishes her mother had cooked, questions poured out: "Where is your hometown in China? What was China like when you were little?"

Her mother spoke of 1937. "Grandpa and Grandma were refugees," she whispered. "The Japanese army invaded. They drove people from their homes and killed so many."

To Iris, it sounded like a legend.

"It was not a legend," her mother said. "It was the Nanjing Massacre."

Iris listened, freezing in shock. In her mind, she saw her ancestral land being devoured like a mulberry leaf. She saw the Yangtze River stained red with blood.

Iris ran to the public library to read more about the Nanjing Massacre—but she couldn't find a single book. On the shelves were rows of books about the Holocaust in Europe, yet there was nothing about the massacre committed by the Japanese army in Nanjing.

How could such history be missing?

A seed of doubt was planted in little Iris's heart. Once touched by rain, it would quickly sprout.

Stories buried in history need those who care to uncover them and tell the world.

Iris was fascinated by the power of words. In middle school, she revived a magazine called *The Maverick*. The name suited her independent spirit perfectly.

But she also loved the clear logic of computers. She worked as a junior programmer, coding the future.

In her yearbook, she bridged her two worlds:

*"Imagination is more important than knowledge." (Einstein)*
*"Poetry is the most beautiful mode of saying things." (Arnold)*

She was sharpening a mind that was both logical and lyrical.

At the University of Illinois, Iris made a bold move. She realized her heart belonged to writing, not coding. So she traded the safe path of computer science for the adventure of journalism.

Her parents stood by her. "Interest is the best teacher," they believed.

Iris flourished. She used her scientific mind to make complex ideas clear. She loved the freedom to explore. "Choices, choices, choices!" she wrote. "That's what I like about it—hearing different opinions."

She had found her voice. The best path, she learned, is the one you choose for yourself.

Inside
Scientists
to map
om
ology
e forms

After college, Iris found her journalism work unsatisfying. She decided to pursue a master's degree in writing at Johns Hopkins University—and soon received an invitation to write a biography of Qian Xuesen, the "Father of China's Missile Program." Though she had no background in this field, she accepted the challenge fearlessly and devoted herself fully.

Throughout the year, she traveled constantly, visiting places like the US National Archives to research Qian's years in America. Once, she even forgot the closing time and was locked inside the archive. Luckily, a night guard heard her calls for help. It became a small episode in her intense, obsessive work.

Summer, 1993. Iris flew to China alone.

She retraced the scientist's steps through Hangzhou, Shanghai, and Beijing. She climbed the Great Wall—finally standing on the dragon she had once traced on her grandfather's map.

"Incredible," she wrote home.

She named her biography *Thread of the Silkworm*—honoring the scientist's patient dedication, spinning his legacy thread by thread.

But it was also her own thread. She was learning that writing wasn't just telling stories. It was weaving the truth.

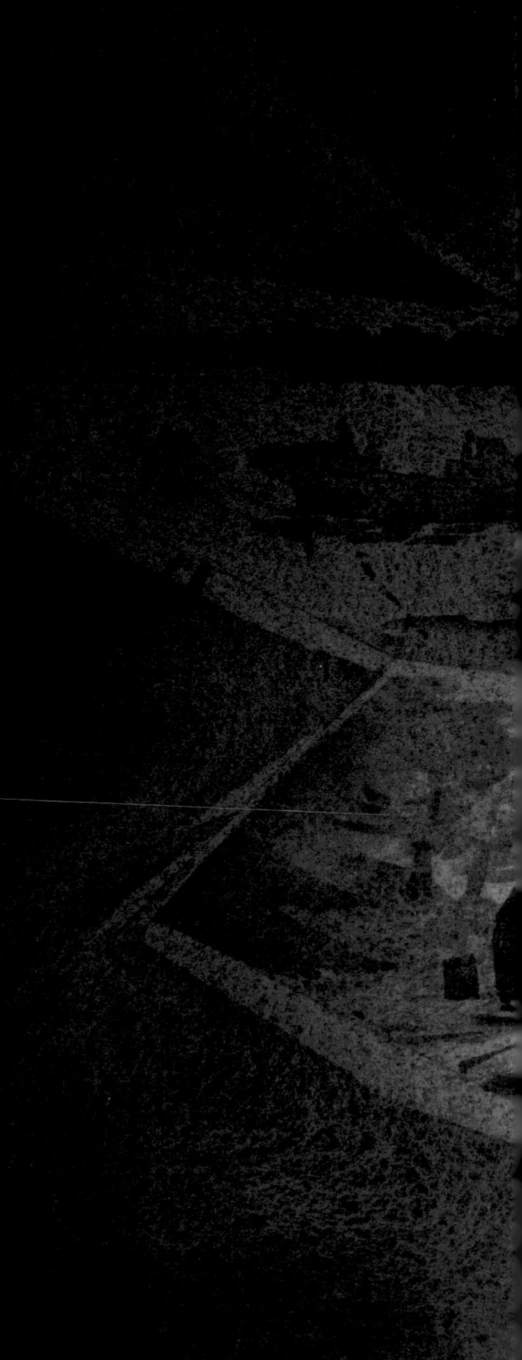

*Thread of the Silkworm* earned acclaim. Iris was now a published author.
But something was missing. What story did she truly need to tell?
Then she saw the photos. Nanjing Massacre. The black-and-white horror left her breathless.
She grabbed the phone. “Mom, I must write this. The victims have no voice!”
Justice was her thread—and now she had found the story that mattered most.

Iris spun a new thread—a thread of truth. She scoured archives for lost voices. Then she found it: The diary of Minnie Vautrin.

As she read, tears fell. Minnie was also a daughter of Illinois. She, too, had walked the halls of their university. In 1937, Minnie stood at the gates of Ginling College, shielding 10,000 lives from the Japanese invaders.

Iris felt a spirit reaching out across time.

You protected them then, she promised. I will protect their memory now.

As Iris combed through buried history, one name stood out—John Rabe, a German who chaired the International Safety Zone Committee and saved countless refugees.

Iris eventually contacted Rabe's granddaughter and uncovered an amazing treasure: John Rabe's diaries.

Written in German across more than a thousand pages, they recorded the atrocities of the Nanjing Massacre in harrowing detail, providing undeniable proof of the Japanese army's crimes.

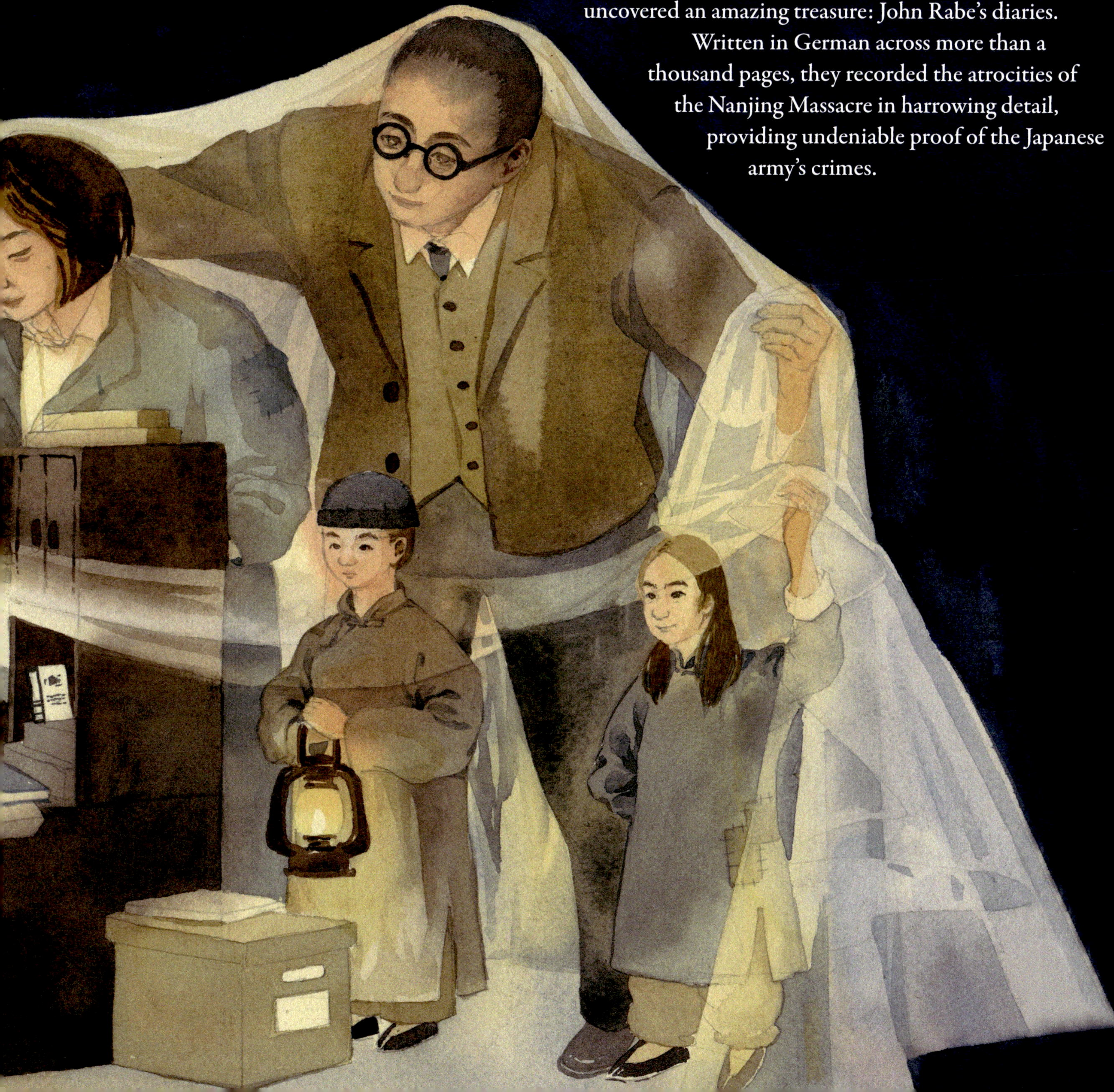

Summer, 1995. Iris returned to Nanjing. Her first trip was wonder; this one was grief.

The city was a "furnace," boiling with summer heat. But Iris pushed on. She walked the sweltering streets to trace the scars of 1937.

She stood at the gates of Ginling College, where Minnie Vautrin had once stood guard.

The sun beat down on her, but the weight in her heart was heavier. She was walking through fire to find the truth.

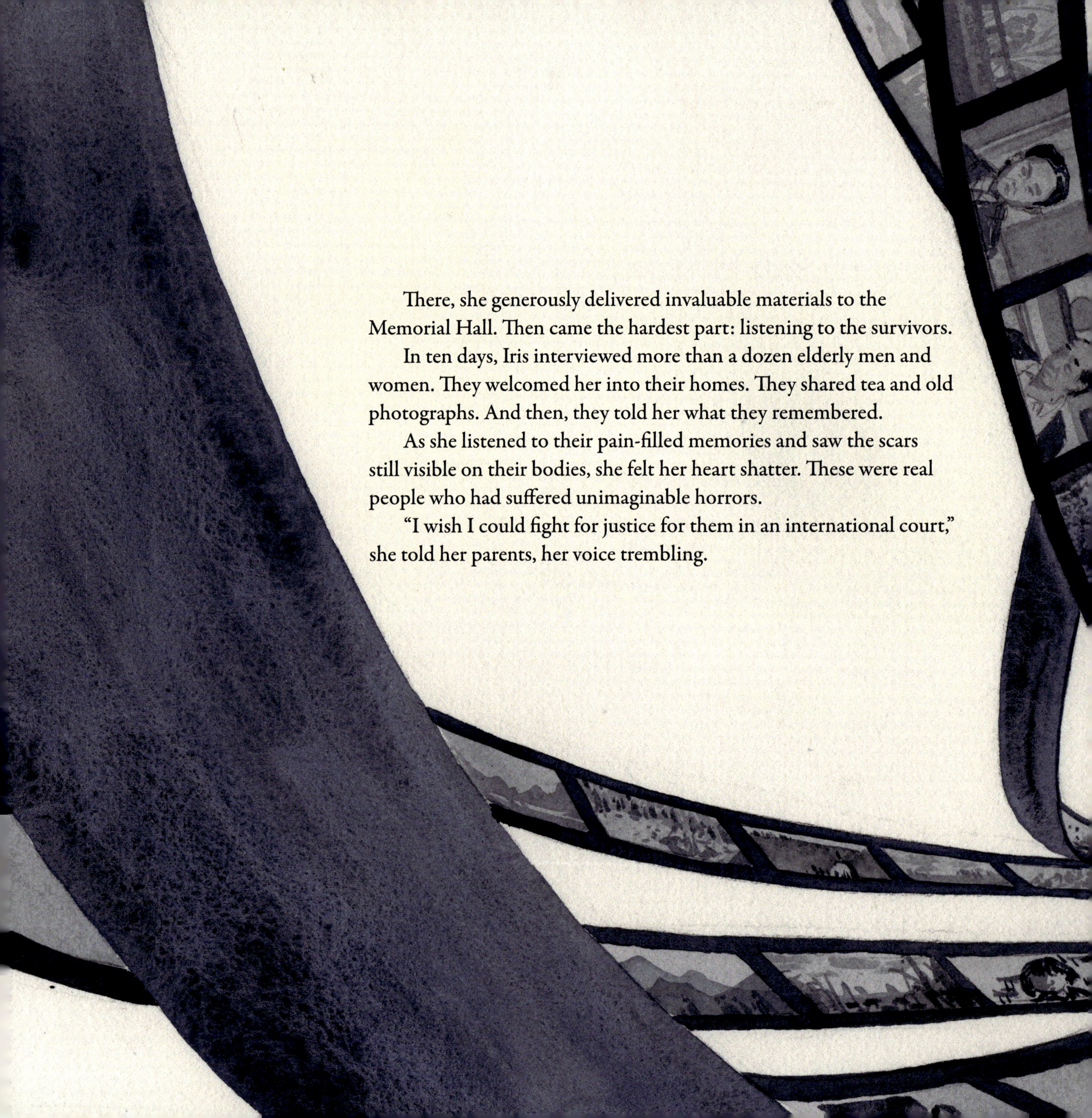

There, she generously delivered invaluable materials to the Memorial Hall. Then came the hardest part: listening to the survivors.

In ten days, Iris interviewed more than a dozen elderly men and women. They welcomed her into their homes. They shared tea and old photographs. And then, they told her what they remembered.

As she listened to their pain-filled memories and saw the scars still visible on their bodies, she felt her heart shatter. These were real people who had suffered unimaginable horrors.

"I wish I could fight for justice for them in an international court," she told her parents, her voice trembling.

Back in America, her study became a fortress of memory. Boxes of documents lined the walls. Video recordings filled the shelves. Survivor interviews covered her desk.

Day and night, Iris pored over these blood-and-tear-stained materials. She forgot to sleep. She forgot to eat.

Her mother called, her voice tight with worry. “Can you endure this? Must you go on?”

“Yes, Mom. I must,” Iris answered. “I must rescue the victims from forgotten history. I must speak for the voiceless dead.”

Her parents became her anchors.

Every draft, they read carefully. Every fact, they checked thoroughly. They drew on their own memories—her mother's childhood in wartime China, her father's scientific precision. Together, they worked late into the night, choosing the right words.

Their support reminded her she wasn't carrying this burden alone.

On her desk, purple irises bloomed quietly. Night after night, the flowers kept watch as her fingers flew across the keyboard.

Click-clack-click. The sound of history being written. The sound of silence being broken.

December 1997. The 60th Anniversary of the Nanjing Massacre.

Iris placed her masterpiece on the table: *The Rape of Nanking*.

It hit the world like a thunderclap. It was the first time the full story was told in English. The book stayed on the bestseller list for months, waking the world from a sixty-year sleep.

Iris's warning rang out to every generation: "Those who cannot remember the past are condemned to repeat it."

Iris became a public warrior. She faced cameras, critics, and even death threats. But she never backed down. On live TV, she debated the Japanese ambassador. She demanded an apology. She demanded dignity.

Her truth broke through the clouds of denial like sunlight after a storm.

Her fight didn't end there. She wrote *The Chinese in America* to prove that her people helped build this country. "I care about justice," she said. Her pen was her sword, and she wielded it for the truth.

She returned to her high school, a hero. Standing at the podium, she shared her greatest secret with the students.

"Please, believe in the POWER OF ONE." "One person can make an enormous difference. You can change millions of lives."

Then, she looked down at her parents. "Mom, Dad," she said softly. "You believed in me from Day One. You are my best friends."

Her parents watched through tears. They didn't just see a famous author. They saw the little girl who took her first wobbly steps on the spring lawn. Now, she was a warrior, striding forward to change the world.

November 9, 2004. The brightest star faded into the night.

Iris had gazed into history's darkness for too long. The weight of millions of sorrows exhausted her spirit. She was only thirty-six.

Her mother—who had survived the bombs of Chongqing, who had cheered her daughter's first steps on that Princeton lawn—now held Iris's books close to her heart.

But the light Iris kindled will never go dark. People honored her with a poem: "A chivalrous woman, writing truth with an iron pen; / A pure heart, comforting the souls of the wronged."

She lived up to her names.

Shun-Ru: Pure and Innocent.

Iris: The eye that sees truth. The flower that blooms with hope. The rainbow that appears after the storm.

Now, the baton passes to you.

Never underestimate the POWER OF ONE. One person can change the world.

Take the pen. Shine the light. Be the rainbow after the darkness.

## *Words to Know*

**Ginling College**
Women's college in Nanjing founded in 1915; during the Nanjing Massacre, American Dean Minnie Vautrin sheltered ~10,000 lives; now part of Nanjing Normal University.

**The Holocaust**
The genocide of six million Jewish people by Nazi Germany (1939–1945).

**Nanjing Massacre**
A six-week period of mass murder by the Japanese military in Nanjing beginning in December 1937; an estimated 200,000 to 300,000 civilians and POWs were killed.

**Qian Xuesen (1911–2009)**
"Father of Chinese Rocketry"; persecuted in the US during the McCarthy era; returned to China to lead missile/space programs.

**John Rabe (1882–1950)**
German businessman who led the International Safety Zone in Nanjing in 1937; his diary provided crucial evidence of war crimes.

**Minnie Vautrin (1886–1941)**
American educator, acting president of Ginling College; sheltered thousands during the Nanjing Massacre (subject of *The Sheltering Tree*, book 2).

## *The Journey of Iris Chang (1968–2004)*

*The Lamp of Truth*

| | |
|---|---|
| March 28, 1968 | Born in Princeton, New Jersey. |
| 1969 | Moved to Champaign, Illinois. |
| 1985 | Entered the University of Illinois. |
| 1987 | Switched major from computer science to journalism. |
| 1989 | Graduated; began career as journalist. |
| 1993 | First trip to China; researched *Thread of the Silkworm*. |
| 1995 | Traveled to Nanjing; interviewed massacre survivors. |
| November 1997 | Published *The Rape of Nanking*; became an international bestseller. |
| 1998 | Debated with the Japanese ambassador on national television. |
| 2003 | Published *The Chinese in America*. |
| November 9, 2004 | Passed away in Santa Clara, California. |
| 2017–2019 | Memorial sites established in China and California to honor her legacy. |

## *Selected Bibliography*


Chang, Iris. *The Chinese in America: A Narrative History*. New York: Viking, 2003.

———. *The Rape of Nanking: The Forgotten Holocaust of World War II*. New York: Basic Books, 1997.

———. *Thread of the Silkworm*. New York: Basic Books, 1995.

Chang, Ying-Ying. *The Woman Who Could Not Forget: Iris Chang Before and Beyond "The Rape of Nanking."* New York: Pegasus Books, 2011.

Li, Peter, ed. *Japanese War Crimes: The Search for Justice*. New Brunswick, NJ: Transaction Publishers, 2003.

Vautrin, Minnie. *Terror in Minnie Vautrin's Nanjing: Diaries and Correspondence, 1937–38*. Edited by Suping Lu. Urbana: University of Illinois Press, 2008.

## *About the Author*

TAN FENGXIA is a Hans Christian Andersen Award Juror (2024, 2026) and Professor of Children's Literature at Nanjing Normal University, China.

As one of the world's leading scholars of children's books, she has devoted her career to bringing Chinese stories to young readers everywhere. She has been a research fellow at Cambridge University and the International Youth Library in Munich.

*The Iris Blooms* is her tribute to the courageous seekers of truth who refuse to let history be forgotten.

Tan Fengxia believes every child deserves to see themselves as a hero of history.

## *About the Illustrator*

LIANG PEILING is an acclaimed watercolor artist and educator. She holds both a bachelor's and a master's degree in painting from the Hubei Institute of Fine Arts. Her evocative artwork has been selected for numerous national exhibitions in China.

Her representative picture books include *Dreaming of Mount Tianmu* (based on the classic poem by Li Bai). She currently serves on the faculty at the South China Business College of Guangdong University of Foreign Studies.

For *The Iris Blooms*, she uses a fluid, emotive watercolor style to capture the delicate balance between the innocence of childhood and the weight of history.